COLORS OF

France

AA Publishing

Author: Laurence Phillips

Produced by AA Publishing

Published by AA Publishing (a trading name of Automobile Association
Developments Limited, whose registered office is Southwood East, Apollo Rise,
Farnborough, Hampshire, GU14 0JW; registered number 1878835).

ISBN 0-7495-4237-3

A01958

A CIP catalogue record for this book is available from the British Library.

Printed and bound in China

COLORS OF

France

CONT

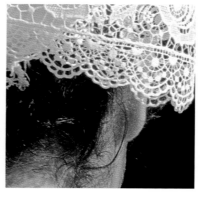

ENTS

COLORS OF **FRANCE**

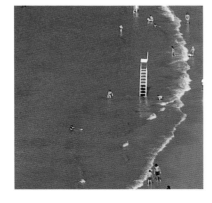

INTROD

COLORS OF FRANCE: **INTRODUCTION**

Take the best that nature can offer and entrust it into the care of a people more than content to cherish it. That is the simple secret of France's dazzling diversity. France was born on one of Creation's better days. A hexagon set between two seas, and as contrasting a selection of mountain ranges as anyone would wish for. The extravagance of the landscape is at once a dramatic gesture and a humble sharing of a panoply of colors, climates, and sensations.

This variety, the sultry Mediterranean and the wild tempestuous Atlantic, the lush Ardennes forests to the north and the rugged corniche cliff-faces in the south, Pyrenean peaks of the west and Alpine tiers to the east, has been divided over the years mostly by the natural boundaries of rivers and mountains, but also by kings and soldiers, revolutionaries and emperors into dukedoms and regions, counties and administrative departments—each corner guarding an identity all its own.

To most people, 'France' means the region and the season in which they first discovered the country. The spot where they first sat by a river tearing chunks from a crusty loaf of bread, the wine cellar where they first sipped a robust red in the company of the family that picked the grapes, or the city square where a smile and greeting from a stranger led to an unplanned conversation that continued late into the night.

A second visit, and a third, lets you start to rationalize and compare. Snapshots and memories redefine the many angles and sides of this hexagon with so many more than six faces. Cycling along empty canal paths under a lazy, leafy canopy is summer in the Midi, just as mulled wine, *pain d'épice* (gingerbread) and hand-carved gifts outside Strasbourg's cathedral is Christmas in Alsace, waiters stacking chairs on tables before dawn to the soft sound of an accordion is Montmartre in November, and a late spring breeze chilling bare arms in the sunlight is a moment of poignant remembrance on the D-Day beaches of Normandy. These categories are, of course, subjective. More universally, however, nothing highlights the happy contrast between French regions better than market day.

Markets and Produce

In Provence the aroma of olives and dried herbs begins streets away from the big open market of Aix, and sunlight bounces off countless bright yellow ceramic bowls. Even ports have their regional difference. The slight salt-pinch of St-Malo's morning air comes from baskets of oysters and mussels. In Nice, mini-rainbows hover above the sheen of fresh fish, fragranced by mimosa and lavender on Cours Salleya. Moving inland, Brittany's hunger pangs are satisfied by sweet and savory crêpes

7

prepared at the roadside, Lyon's stalls are draped with curtains of hanging sausages and game, while in Rouen a flea market selling new shoes and clothes peters naturally into a food fair, with farmhouse cheeses, *pain d'épice,* and bottles of cider. All this produce is an ever-present reminder that despite, and because of, their many differences, every region loves its lunch.

As much as the landscape, it is food that defines each region, and discovering the infinite variety is an adventure in itself: trickling off your itinerary and coming by chance across a country strawberry fair in the north, or an olive market in the south; happening upon monks tending their vines in a walled *clos* (cloister); filling cupped palms, and any spare bottles, with mineral water in a spa resort; or watching the morning catch spill from the nets onto the fishing wharf.

This delightful diversity reflects France's strong regional identity. When a Frenchman talks of *mon pays* (my country), he is more likely to be referring to the area in which he grew up than to the nation as a whole. So Normandy remains resolutely Norman, Brittany defiantly Breton, and the villages of the south decidedly contrary. Every town has its local hero, be it a literary or military figure (duly honored with a museum), a local craft or tradition (duly honored with a museum), or at the very least a local eccentric (duly honored with a museum).

So the newly arrived baker from another region beyond the hills will be regarded as more of a foreigner than the welcome visitor from another country, clutching a map and mouthing unfamiliar phrases. Naturally, regional pride guarantees that shopkeepers, restaurateurs, and even the old man playing *pétanque* on a dusty village square will upgrade the welcome if only to prove that their region is the only true France.

Local Pride

For pride and contentment are the keys to France's infinite variety. Since every French person knows for certain that he or she lives in the most beautiful and richest corner of the land, no-one has any time for excessive homogenization. The blue, white, and red *tricouleur* may fly above the town hall, to be saluted and applauded on Bastille Day (July 14) and other state occasions, but for the villager, the label on his wine bottle is just as important a standard; and, in any case, the land itself creates its own cultural identity.

Volcanoes in Auvergne provided the black stone that built the cathedral of Clermont-Ferrand. These same rocks filtered the mineral water that stirred into existence dozens of elegant spas, and nurtures the wild mountain flowers on the green hilltops that flavor the milk to make the creamiest St-Nectaire cheese.

Along the Loire, the removal of the soft, creamy white *tufeau* stone, quarried to build chateaus, left a system of artificial caves that evolved into troglodyte villages. Similarly, the waterlogged

France is a land of magnificent chateaus. The best way to appreciate the Château de Villandry (above), according to locals, is to visit four times: in spring, summer, fall, and winter to experience the transformations in the striking Renaisssance-style gardens.

marshlands of Picardie and the north gave birth to floating market gardens in St-Omer and Amiens that yield endive as crisp, yellow, and refreshing as any Chardonnay. And an island in the Seine became Paris, and nature, thus tamed, nurtured art. Art in its turn never stopped taking its cue from those very resources that shaped France itself.

Artists and Heroes

Flying buttresses rising from the sea, those cliffs at Etretat in Normandy, thrown into stark relief by the watery grays and shades of the northern skies, inspired a generation of Impressionists from Claude Monet to Alfred Sisley. Likewise, the south's crystal blue light shot with spun gold illuminated the canvasses of Vincent van Gogh, Henri Matisse, and Paul Cézanne.

Of course it was human nature that nudged Henri de Toulouse Lautrec and Edgar Degas to their respective other worlds of dance in Paris. Nonetheless, across the country, each town is proud to declare its natural or adopted son: Valenciennes has Jean-Antoine Watteau, Montauban parades Jean-Auguste Ingres, Nice boasts Marc Chagall, and even Amboise, home of kings and princes, sports its association with Leonardo da Vinci (he died there).

Lionization is not a strictly male preserve. France is just as proud of its women. The west in particular boasts a roll-call of feisty heroines, from Joan of Arc in Rouen, through the serial child-

Shop for your evening meal in true French style by visiting the local market, whether you're in Nice (pictured left) on the Côte d'Azur, in the busy streets of Paris (above right), or in a remote mountain village. After, sit in an outdoor café and watch French life unfold before you.

bride Anne of Brittany, and all those lethal Loire chatelaines (Diane de Poitiers and Catherine de' Medici among them) to the mother of all queen mothers, Eleanor of Aquitaine, buried alongside her favorite son Richard the Lionheart at Fontevraud Abbey in Anjou.

If so many prodigal sons and daughters were not reason enough to raise a glass or several in a toast to absent friends, France can always be relied upon to find a good excuse to wield the corkscrew. Even then, do not expect just any old wine. When the locals reach for a bottle they are offering you a taste of the *terroir*.

Soil and Wine

As buzzwords go, *terroir* is one of the best in the business. Never mind the dictionary definition (it means soil), *terroir* is what makes every wine different from its neighbor harvested in the next valley. The very essence of that other catch-all phrase *'je ne sais quoi,'* *terroir* is the indefinable ingredient that a wine gets from its own soil, its home town, and the sweat and toil of the people whose lives are dedicated to raising and nurturing the grape from the vine to the bottle.

Every region claims that its *terroir* makes its wines special. And, whether you are talking about a *grand cru* from one of the better houses in Bordeaux or a simple table wine from a co-op by the foothills of the Pyrénées, it will be special to the locals, since age-old family recipes will have been created around the particular flavors of the tipple.

So, if eating barbecued mussels at a Languedoc *brasucade* (barbecue) opt for a humble local *vin de pays* rather than a pricier or more exotic Bordeaux. Likewise, stick with a good Burgundy with

It's no wonder France is known for its gourmet chefs—the diverse climate allows the country to produce an appetizing range of food: mouth-watering creams, cheeses, and butters from Normandy; olive oil, garlic, and clumps of wild herbs from Provence; truffles from the southwest.

your *boeuf bourguignon*. The one exception to the rule is of course champagne—to be celebrated anywhere, at any time.

Since the French have a weakness for Life, with a capital L, ideally served with a bottle of something special, it is no surprise that summer in France comes with a musical soundtrack.

Music and Festivals

Provençal crickets are seduced into submission by world-class sopranos; cooing, wooing pigeons in an abbey cloister are spurred on by the romantic trills and spills of a gifted pianist; and the breeze of a beach pine-grove is electrified by the sunset syncopations of a jazz legend.

Since mealtimes are unrestrained by the clock, and lunch can stretch from midday until it segues into a *p'tit apéro* before dinner, likewise the concept of summer is also granted the same elasticity. The estival (summer) festival season may officially begin on July 14 and continue until the *rentrée* (the last weekend before back to school in September), but in truth, France is willing to picnic and party under the stars for far longer than that.

The season really kicks off at apple blossom time in April with *Jazz Sous les Pommiers*, music around the calvados orchards at Coutances, an excuse to sip farmhouse cider and tap your feet late into the night. It lasts until Burgundy's final winemaking festivals of late autumn, drinking new Nuits St. Georges around an old wine-press and toasting a job well done.

It seems that there are as many excuses for a festival as there are for a drink, and no matter how small or how powerful the town, village, or city, France is ever ready to declare a party. The grand set pieces of Provence are big-budget blowouts, with pageant-scale operas staged in the Roman theater of Orange, a temporary open-air opera house erected in the heart of Aix-en-Provence, and the Avignon International Festival, a major arts event.

While Nice and Juan-Les-Pins host the big names of international jazz and blues for the wealthy Riviera set, music lovers may find a legend of equal stature at their local village event.

The Périgord Noir festival in sleepy, rural Dordogne fills village churches with renowned classical musicians playing from moonrise until the small hours. Elsewhere, a New Orleans legend might settle in for the night in a garden in Marciac. The Pierre Boulez Festival at St-Etienne is quite likely

to produce the London Symphony Orchestra in a suburban sports hall.

The lure, for artists as much as audiences, is the infectious native pride of each region. Since festivals celebrate the local produce and skills as much as the talent of the guests, a winegrowing village will pull its corks long after the final encore, a fishing port may serve a communal banquet that threatens to run into breakfast, and even a town with no agricultural specialty of its own will remember a family recipe to be dished out well into the night.

The line between produce, tradition, and the arts is easily blurred, just as a solemn unveiling of a new wine in a little-known wine cooperative dissolves from speechifying, through a chestnut- or olive-tasting session, into hardcore head-banging as a local band takes the stage, during the 50 or so late autumn festivals to launch the *vin primeur* (first wine of the season) in Hérault. The triennial Marionette Festival in the Ruritanian Ardennes town of Charleville-Mézières begins with workshops and ends with the puppet equivalent of jam sessions in bars and the streets.

History plays its part. *Son et lumière* shows, especially around the Loire, tell the stories of chateaus and their inhabitants, with fabulous special effects. Around sites associated with Frédéric Chopin (such as his lover George Sand's home at Nohant) summer brings piano recitals. Some areas enjoy a less structured format. The legendary violinist Yehudi Menuhin (1916–1999) created the Flâneries d'Eté in the champagne city of Reims, a summer season of some 90 free concerts hidden around town.

All over France, the weekend around June 21 brings National Music Day, when the entire nation celebrates, from the smallest village to cosmopolitan cities, and free concerts merge with café entertainers and impromptu sessions until barrels and throats become dry well past everybody's bedtime.

It may be too dark to see the subtle shades of the rocks and the trees and the effect of the sunlight on the water; but at this time of night, with the echo of a song in your heart and the aftertaste of fine food and wine lingering in your mouth, the hexagon with a million sides shares the infinite colors of pure *bonhomie*.

France loves its festivals and they are guaranteed to be colorful spectacles, like this flower-filled parade in Nice (above left). And how better to celebrate than with a glass of the local wine? French wine is a matter of national and regional pride. Pictured right is Château de la Graves, Bordeaux.

FLAVORS

COLORS OF FRANCE: **FLAVORS**

1

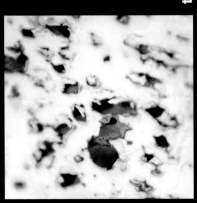

F rance is an assault on all the senses. The eyes have it easy—panoramas, vistas, and improbable beauty simply unfold in front of them—but the nostrils and the tastebuds are assailed and surrender to stimulation at every turn. Each region brings its own particular flavor (or *saveur*).

In the south, it may be sharp twists and tangs of herbs, lavender, rosemary, and thyme infusing every mouthful. In the heartland, the strong scents of goats' and ewes' cheese fills the air in the fields as much as the restaurants. In Normandy, apple blossom, calvados, and cider season the breezes and stir the appetite. And everywhere, every single day is kick-started at dawn, boosted at noon, and revived at dusk by the heady aroma of freshly ground coffee.

Every café is familiar, yet every café is unique, from the chic, sleek, sharp designs of a Parisian café where smart media types air kiss and flip their latest cell phones, to the PMU (Pari Mutuel Urbain where you can place your horse-racing bets off-course) sports bars, where men with moustaches tear up betting slips and order another drink without averting their gaze from the omnipresent TV relaying horseracing and soccer.
In the smallest country town, the bar on the main square opposite the *mairie* (town hall) and church, will be the central meeting place for the day, from a breakfast coffee taken standing up at the bar to a noonday beer and *plat du jour* lunch, newspaper or a paperback book propped up against the salt and pepper shakers, to an after-work social buzz, and a late night winding-down after dinner at the restaurant across the way.

CAFÉ CULTURE

Meanwhile the Café de la Gare, outside the railroad station will be the meeting point for the youth of the town. Whatever the current fashions, expect to find a handful of teens in the timeless uniform of white T-shirt and faded denims, gathered around a motorbike and making one drink last for hours.

FRENCH BREAD

Campagne
Poids
400g
Prix au kg
3 €5
1 €30

2 €50

Previous page: A long drink as an endless
afternoon turns into an everlasting evening. A
glass of wine, a pastis, or a refreshing *menthe à
l'eau* accompany the permanent parade of passers-
by that makes people-watching from a harbor café
in St-Tropez such a delight.

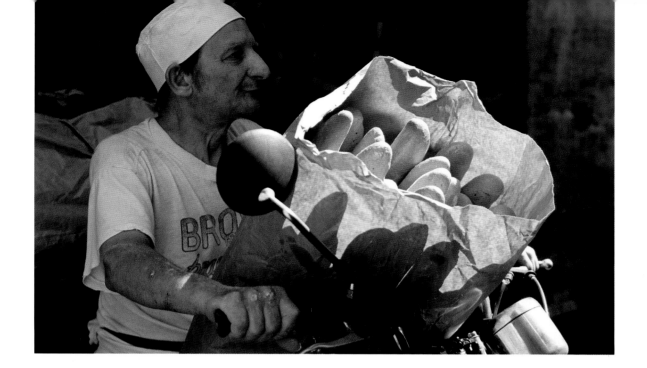

An art form in itself, French bread's myriad shapes, sizes, and textures offer so much more than the clichéd image of the long baguette; but baguettes and flutes, tucked under the arm fresh from the oven, or gathered in the sack-load by early evening waiters collecting the night's supply from their restaurant's nearest bakery, these are everyday accompaniments to a meal.

Other loaves—*pain de campagne*, with crusts that could defy a chainsaw, multigrain *céreale* bread or wholemeal *pain complet*—are stacked on the highest shelf of the bakery. Every region has its specialty. In the south, twisted *fougasse* rings are pumped full of olives, ham, and cheese, for tearing with the teeth and the fingers long before you get home. In Paris, the master bakery Poilâne creates loaves that great chefs regard with the kind of awe that is usually reserved for truffles and foie gras.

MARKETS

On market day, France wears its heart on its sleeve and each region sets out its wares. Along the allée Paul-Riquet, Béziers' grand tree-lined promenade, waiters dodge traffic to bring hot food and chilled wine from cafés to lazy lunchers in the shade during Friday's flower market. Cascades of jasmine, gushes of iris, willowy lilies, and billowing baskets of trailing plants share floor space with cages of exotic birds, crates of ducklings, and trays of baby rabbits.

Some markets are invisible. The truffle markets of Drôme exist entirely in the eye contact made between chefs with money to buy the black diamonds and men with deep coat-pockets to store the surreptitiously gathered and traded delights. A nod, a chink of glasses in a café and the deal is done.

By contrast, most Provence markets flourish huge terracotta and wicker bowls of olives, sacks of herbs, and plaited tresses of garlic. Mirabelle plums and bottles of the fruit's liqueur with jars of allied jams weigh down the trestles of Lorraine, while in the north, markets are a shop window for plump heads of endive, ripe artichokes, and the succulent salad leaves of the region's market gardens. But the display does not stop there. Lille's Wazemmes market combines antiques and bric-à-brac, puppies and kittens, new potatoes and old saucepans with rôtisseries turning corn-fed, free-range chickens, dripping their juices on sliced potatoes and onions beneath the spits. Stallholders stand by vast pans, itemizing their wares, lingering over recipes: paella or couscous ('fresh mutton, not just lamb, and spicy sausage as well'); perhaps mussels ('breadcrumbs and fresh herbs').

WINE MAKING

Unending vistas of neatly landscaped vines mark the seasons of France: winter, with the whiff of charred wood as old stock is burned off; spring, when the first shoots begin to turn the sorry-looking twigs into plants; and summer, when the vineyards are resplendent in their greenery.

Then, the early fall, as the russets and reds tinge those leaves, a signal for the harvesters to begin the back-breaking ritual of the harvest, cutting tools in hands as gnarled as the vines, filling pails and baskets with precious cargo to be tipped into trucks and taken to the wineries.

In the chalk wine cellars of Champagne, hidden from the light of the changing seasons, champagne masters perform the never-ending *remouage*, delicately turning by degrees bottles perched in easel-like racks, to make sure that the sediment from fermentation is deposited against the cork.

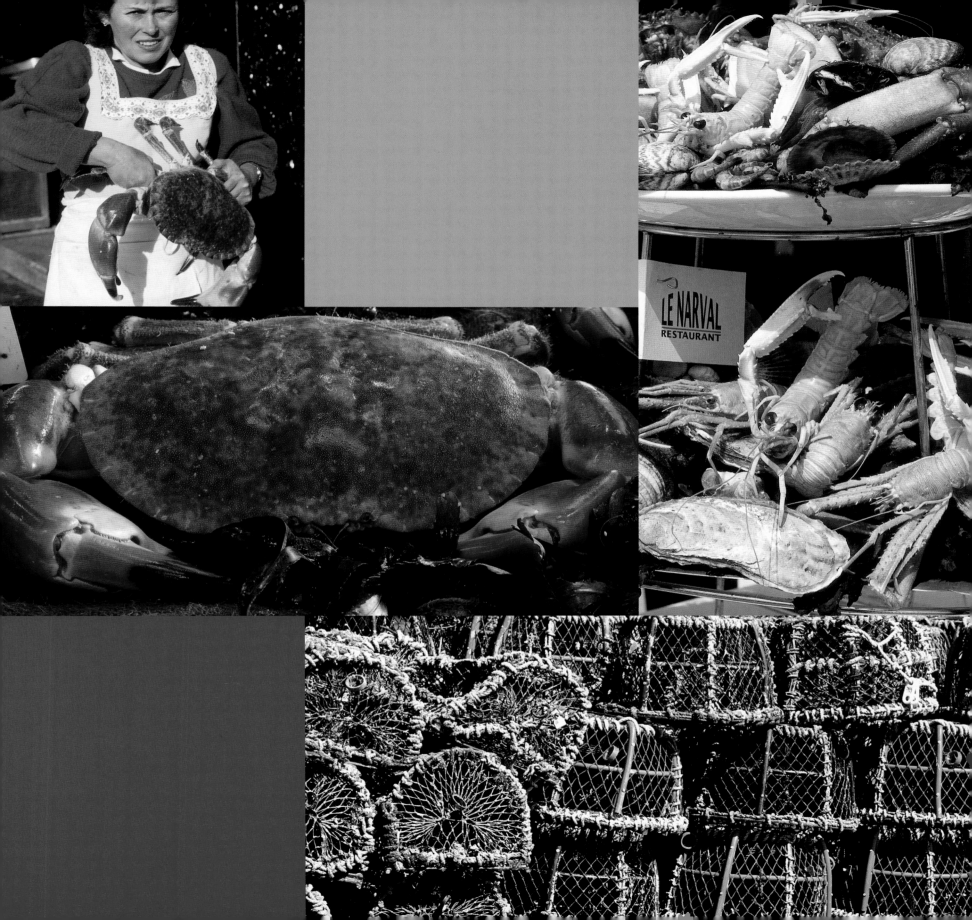

Previous page: A luxury in the city, but in the
coastal villages of France the stuff of daily
sustenance. Seafood and crustaceans—crabs,
lobster, mussels, and oysters—casually sold on the
waterfront, lovingly savored in the sunset.

CHOCOLATES

With rainbow colors to give the lie to the rules of milk, dark, and white, chocolates have fillings even more diverse than the improbable hues in which they are dressed. Originally dispensed from pharmacies, quality chocolates and candy are even now selected and packed with the same care one would expect from a quality jeweler. Chocolates are divided into ganaches and truffles and the exotic fillings may range from crème fraîche, alcohol, and fruits to such bizarre specialties as Roquefort cheese and olives, created by master *chocolatier* Guy Bouzigues of Pomerols.

In Parisian boutiques such as Debauve et Gallais, whose famous clients have included Louis XVI and Marcel Proust, customers select their own choices to be placed with care in dainty *ballotin* boxes, and sold by weight.

CHEESE

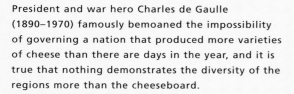

President and war hero Charles de Gaulle (1890–1970) famously bemoaned the impossibility of governing a nation that produced more varieties of cheese than there are days in the year, and it is true that nothing demonstrates the diversity of the regions more than the cheeseboard.

Roquefort, the queen of blue cheeses (above left) is made from ewes' milk and matured in the caves of the Massif Central. Legend has it that the distinctive veins of bread mold originate from the day a shepherd boy left a cheese sandwich under a rock by a stream while chasing his girlfriend.

Camembert (above), the best-known of Normandy's delicious dairy products, is rich and creamy, thanks to excellent pastures; other delights from the region include Livarot and Pont-l'Evêque. The local butter, Beurre d'Isigny, is also recognized as the best in France.

TOMME
D'ABONDANCE
AU LAIT CRU
LE KG. 15.€00 98.3°

Spot the best farmhouse cheeses in markets and specialist stores, as they are sold unwrapped on a bed of straw. *Chèvres* (goats' cheeses), rich and flavorsome, or subtle and mild, rolled in ash for spreading on bread, or formed into small *crottin* cakes for cooking and serving on fresh salad leaves.

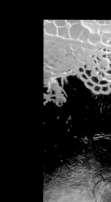

Taciturn the French may be in public, but this very characteristic has inspired generations of writers and some of the most heart-warming and affecting tales of the land and the people who love it. Such mute eloquence tells the most poignant and vivid love stories. A sunny day in Paris brings a thousand and one romances, the only soundtrack the sudden breezes rustling leaves on the avenues, boulevards, and banks of the Seine, the George Gershwin toot of taxi horns, and the inevitable sound of an accordion from a sidewalk café. The capital was designed to be discovered two-by-two—parks and parterres with convenient benches, balustrades, and corners for ignoring the view. Fountains in the Jardins des Tuileries make a splashing, refreshing background for a kiss just yards from the bustling rue de Rivoli and the crowds lining up to visit the Louvre.

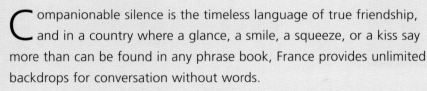

FRIENDS

Companionable silence is the timeless language of true friendship, and in a country where a glance, a smile, a squeeze, or a kiss say more than can be found in any phrase book, France provides unlimited backdrops for conversation without words.

For a nation with such rich and varied language, it is paradoxical that the greatest eloquence is in the shrug. The most abiding of all images: pastel-colored houses clustered around dusty squares, where old men while away the hours sipping pastis on a café *terrasse* and bowling under age-old plane trees.

In summer a new landscape emerges for saying nothing with those you care about. Paris Plage is 2 miles (3.5km) of sandy beach along the right bank of the Seine, where you may throw a Frisbee, play volleyball, or, most likely, doze in a hammock, doing nothing in delicious silence.

The city, and every other town and village in the land, makes for just as comfortable a hang-out for friends as for lovers. Benches and loungers strategically placed in sunshine or in shade do as well as any café terrace for passing an hour or two resetting the body clock to a more civilized time.

Quality time does not have a special window in the diary. A secluded corner on the way back from the shops is as good a place as any for the unscheduled serendipity of appreciating the one you are with.

POSEURS

France à deux may be ideal for concentrating on each other, but a solitary stroll is perfect for people-watching. A suspicious mind might assume that the characters striking their poses at every turn had been supplied by some central casting agency, so easily do they fit the image of France presented for more than a century by movie-makers.

However, the dog as fashion accessory is a reality of life in the city, and every sidewalk becomes a catwalk as the well-heeled turn a well-turned heel and sashay from meeting to meeting, from rendezvous to rendezvous, perfectly aware of the appreciative glances from café tables and those whose working lifestyles do not feature couture and the chance to strut their stuff.

Watching the world go by is an art perfected from the avenue des Champs-Elysées in Paris, to the

Cours Mirabeau in Aix-en-Provence, Les Planches of Deauville to la Croisette in Cannes. France comes with a musical soundtrack and anyone with a saxophone, guitar, or accordion is likely to punctuate and syncopate a street scene or subway journey. On National Music Day in June, or any given Sunday in the park, the French will show their appreciation and take to the makeshift dance floor. Weekends see *guinguettes*, parties at riverside dance halls on the outskirts of a city where workers and their families relax to music. People-watching is a national obsession, but it is not all one-way traffic. The over-the-top matron dressed to kill is not only there to be watched. She may be having just as much fun herself, watching the watchers.

POUR
Le Musée de Céret

Picasso

Céret le 19.9.54.

PICASSO A CÉRET, 1953 © SU

France is something of an artist's model and inspiration. The azure light of the Mediterranean and the south excited and elicited as many masterpieces from the Impressionists as did the grayer skies of Normandy and the north.

From the Place du Tertre in Montmartre to the Pont des Arts wooden footbridge across the Seine to any leafy terrace in a fishing port, artists of all styles and abilities set up their easels and attempt to capture the spirit of the scene.

Each region proudly proclaims its legendary artist in residence. Honfleur, in Normandy, has galleries hung with works by Eugène Boudin (1824–98), mentor of the early Impressionists. Céret, in the Pyrénées, has a museum devoted to the town's discovery by Pablo Picasso (1881–1973).

ARTISTS

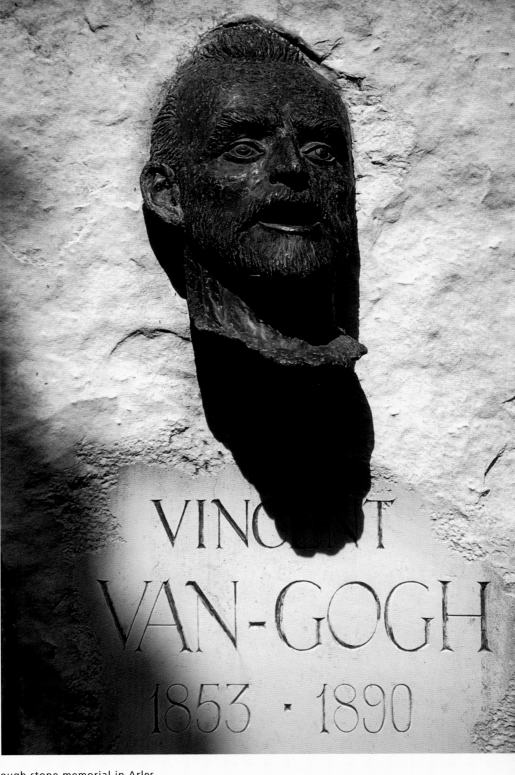

A plaque featuring the artist Paul Cézanne (1839–1906) may be seen in Aix-en-Provence. Visitors can follow a trail of sites painted by and associated with the artist, and the painter's studio remains as he left it.

Sunlight striking the rough stone memorial in Arles pays tribute to the emotionally tortured Vincent van Gogh (1853–1890). The Provençal town is filled with scenes and views immortalized by the artist, who spent several of his final years there, before his untimely death in Auvers-sur-Oise.

A deserted beach at Barneville-Carteret on the
west coast of Normandy's Cotentin peninsula
where an artist prepares to capture the seascape.
The Channel Island of Jersey lies less than 20 miles
(32km) off the coast here.

From the simplicity of the Pyrenean villages, such as the undiscovered modesty of Camurac in the Aude, to the chic sophistication of the Alps, France's five major mountain ranges give the country a vivid winter diversity. The brightly colored clothes of skiers taking the sunshine outside a restaurant in Val d'Isère (above left) show that style matters, whatever the weather. From the peaks to *les plages*: beaches have lured holidaymakers since the mid-19th century. The Empress Eugénie (1826–1920), wife of Emperor Napoleon III and France's first celebrity royal, made Biarritz a fashionable holiday resort, and British and American visitors discovered the Riviera.

LEISURE

The brisk breezes of broad beaches on the Atlantic coasts make them hugely popular with sporting types. Biarritz attracts an energetic crowd as the breakers turn the *plage* into Europe's surfing capital, while along the coast windsurfing, hang-gliding, and kite-flying attract sensation seekers.

Next page: Despite its sporting reputation, Biarritz still attracts those whose idea of leisure is simply to surrender to the sunshine.

RURAL LIFE

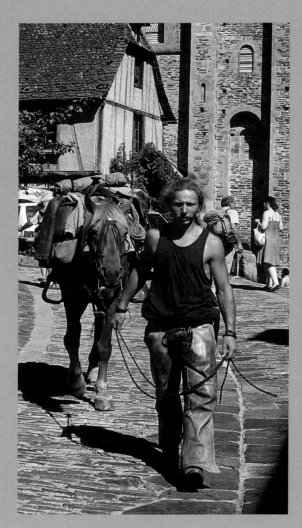

Rural life provides a stark and refreshing contrast to the contemporary cosmopolitan world of the main cities. Country trades, talents, and *métiers* are still passed on through families, much as they were in medieval times.

The family growing olives, chestnuts, or figs will still set out its stall in a weekly market or outside the front door of the family home. Deliveries may be made by donkey or battered decades-old Citroen 2CV van (known colloquially as a *dodosh*). When the donkey dies or the van wheezes its last,

then, and only then, will its replacement be the most modern vehicle.

The comfortable anachronism of ramshackle wooden shutters sealing in modern plastic windows or a horse-drawn delivery cart driven by a youth in Nike sneakers, proves that the village is

not a theme park re-creation but a constantly evolving reality that moves at a civilized pace. A village fête easily accommodates both the old lady singing folk tunes alongside the over-amplified shouts of a local punk band, and the ritual of dressing up in time-worn costumes for a pageant or festival sits well alongside the chinos and denim of those who are merely there for the ride.

Youth and age blend amicably together, with respect shown for the widow who climbs the steep village street to her home after the daily trip to the bakery, and country restaurants filled with Sunday families, three or four generations around the same table.

BRETON

Every corner of France has its own identity, but Brittany is a culture in itself. The kingdom of the Celts, it has been part of France only since the 16th century, and guards its independent identity with pride. Signs and menus are often bilingual, as locals are determined to keep their own language.

The region's Breton name is Armorica, literally, land of the sea, and its fishing and seafaring heritage provides the staple diet of seafood and inspires much of the folk traditions. *Pardons* are pilgrimages with feasting and fun accompanying the blessing of the waters and fishing boats.

These festivals, and the annual summer gathering in Lorient of Celts from across the globe, provide the ideal opportunity to appreciate the charming black-and-white costumes, including the pretty lace *coiffes* (headdresses) that many older women still wear to Mass each Sunday morning.

CTURE 3

COLORS OF FRANCE: **ARCHITECTURE**

MODERNIST

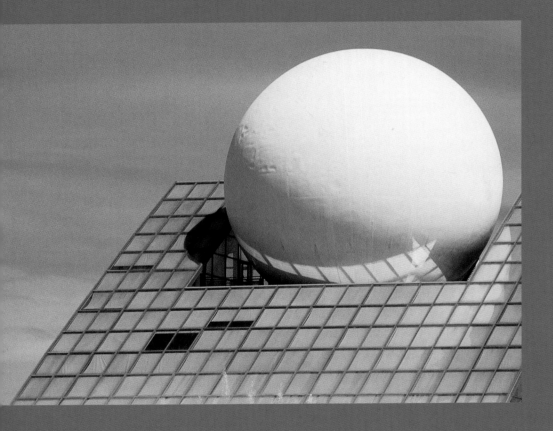

With Roman remains by the score and Renaissance chateaus by the hundred, the French have no intention of turning their country into a vast heritage center.

Before the first brick had been laid in Disneyland Resort Paris's Magic Kingdom, Futuroscope, near Poitiers, the European Park of the Moving Image (above left), had set the architectural style of French theme parks.

The Tour de Crédit Lyonnais (above right), dominating the modern business district in Lille, is affectionately known to locals as the ski-boot.

Designed by Christian de Portzamparc, the tower is part of the modern Euralille district landscaped by the Dutch architect Rem Koolhaas to complement a city of Flemish squares and cobbled streets.

Eyebrows raised at President Mitterand's almost Napoleonic schemes when he launched his Grands Projets (La Défense, the Louvre Pyramid, and his eponymous National Library) in the 1980s, but the monumental gesture predates Napoleon. Ambitious architects are synonymous with great regimes. Vauban's remarkable fortresses defined the age of Louis XIV (1678–1715); Gustave Eiffel's bridges and Tower proclaimed a young Republic at the end of the 19th century. Straddling the millennium, Norman Foster's Millau Viaduct on the A75 highway is a veritable 21st-century Pont du Gard. So a nation self-sufficient in Gothic cathedrals and Romanesque churches, warmly embraces another dramatic architectural gesture for France in the New European age.

From business to leisure, Otto von Spreckelsen's Grande Arche de la Défense (left) in the heart of Paris's financial district, was built for France's bicentenary in 1989. These hotel balconies in la Grande Motte (above) are part of an architectural revival in Languedoc.

Previous page: Inside out. Richard Rogers and Renzo Piano's celebrated Centre Georges Pompidou in Paris upstages most of the works displayed inside this museum of modern art.

Timber-frame buildings mark out some of France's most picturesque corners and historic cities. From the alpine chalets of the east to the postcard-quaint Pays-d'Auge farmhouses and Honfleur's imposing port buildings in the west, this *colombage* (half timbering) ranges from simple

TIMBER FRAME

geometric shapes to ornate patterns, as in these elaborately ornamented housefronts in a square in the heart of old Rennes.

In Strasbourg and the surrounding towns and villages of Alsace, the black-and-white buildings are often bedecked with tubs of red geraniums

and hanging baskets of blue and white lobelia; the tall brick chimney stacks make homes for nesting storks.

The simple monochromes of the walls of the half-timbered houses in the wine-making towns and villages of Burgundy are often complemented by

vivid shiny hues on the roofs, with bright yellow, red, blue, and silver tiles set in intricate designs above the buildings.

DETAILS

It is always worth stepping just that little bit closer to admire the detail in even the simplest rustic farmhouse. A modest doorway at the side of a discreet abbey, such as that in the Béarnaise village of Bielle (above left), may reveal a craftsmanship and a touch of flamboyant Gothic style to rival the grand porch of a cathedral. And windows that are usually shuttered but suddenly revealed on a sunny afternoon in a 15th-century street in the village of Turenne (top) may prove to be real works of art. The leaded glass in perfect proportion encourages the casual passer-by to raise an eye just that little bit higher to appreciate the family coat-of-arms chiseled into the lintel.

A moment's pause, some time to stand and stare, brings its own rewards: a seductive glimpse of the overt extravagance of a Renaissance colonnade or the simple application of bright Provençal paintwork to the shutters in a simple stone cottage, an ornate wrought-iron finishing touch to a window above the city traffic, or the carved face of Marianne, the enduring symbol of the French Republic.

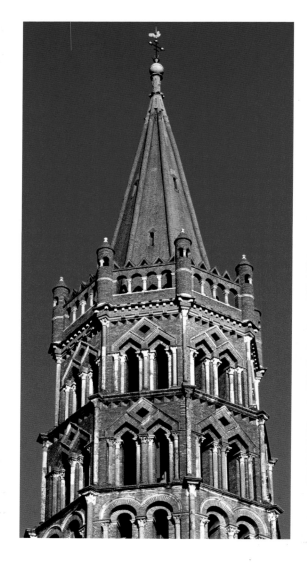

Belfries and towers, spires and turrets are reminders of France's ongoing battle between church and state, the divine and the secular. In cities and towns as diverse as Lyon and Toulouse, Pézenas and Paris, towers tacked on to private houses served two purposes: enclosing staircases and declaring the civic power and wealth of the citizen who lived there.

In the north of France, belfries on churches and town halls jostle for supremacy. Lille's most imposing cathedral-like steeple belongs to the Chamber of Commerce. The belfries were only outranked by mill chimneys when the industrial revolution brought new money into the fray. Lille's textile-manufacturing suburb of Roubaix was known as the town of a thousand chimneys. Many of these factories have long been demolished, but they remain a powerful popular symbol.

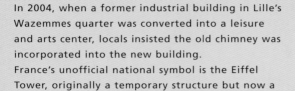

TOWERS

In 2004, when a former industrial building in Lille's Wazemmes quarter was converted into a leisure and arts center, locals insisted the old chimney was incorporated into the new building.
France's unofficial national symbol is the Eiffel Tower, originally a temporary structure but now a

national monument that has garnered as many legends in little over a century as any age-old monolith (the steps climbed on horseback, the lift mechanics sabotaged so that Hitler could not be photographed at the top during wartime Occupation, and so forth).

Religious architecture holds its own too. Although church domes and steeples proliferate, La Mosquée de Paris, (page 66 second left) with its crenellations and Moorish patterns, dominates part of the Left Bank and has secular glamour too (Rita Hayworth married Prince Aly Aga Khan here in 1949).

CHURCHES

Magnificent and awe-inspiring, the grand cathedrals of France are cool reminders of another age. The greatest of an enviable collection of Gothic masterpieces is Notre Dame de Paris (opposite), its rose windows showering those inside with sparkling shades of blue and red light. Built from 1163 to 1345, the cathedral's gargoyle-adorned towers dominate the Paris skyline. Similar Gothic extravagances may be savored across France, from the lofty cathedral at Amiens to the surprisingly squat version in Narbonne, disguised externally to resemble a fortress and so dissuade marauding armies from sacking the city. Yet some of the humblest Romanesque churches and riverside chapels have their treasures. Visitors flock to see the stained-glass windows Marc Chagall created for the tiny chapel in the hamlet of Le Saillant, outside Brive.

CHATEAUS

Cupolas and belfries, towers and spires crown the grandest of all the chateaus of the Loire, Château de Chambord. In a wonderland sprinkled with castles and palaces, this 16th-century Renaissance confection, built for François I, is surely the masterpiece. While such architectural extravagance fueled the imagination of author Charles Perrault (1628–1703), who was inspired to write his fairy tale *The Sleeping Beauty* on a visit to the nearby Château d'Ussé, most were symbols of political power-broking and many served time as working fortresses.

LANDM
& VIEW

ARKS

COLORS OF FRANCE:
LANDMARKS & VIEWS

4

White chalk cliffs in the north, raw ocher in the south, and across the land outcrops of granite, basalt, and limestone rising above rivers and fields dominate the landscape: often topped with castles, fortresses, chapels, and abbeys, clusters of civilization are thrust skyward above the plains and valleys of a land still rugged and raw.

The majesty of the Gorges du Tarn in the Cevennes, where *batalier* boatmen (gondoliers à la français) steer a course between the high upreared fronts of abutting cliff faces at La Malène; hang-gliders launching themselves off the verdant crests of dormant volcanoes in the Auvergne; mariners' wives looking out to sea from Mont St-Clair at Sète; motorists speeding along the corniches of the Riviera; Channel-swimmers guiding themselves toward the twin peaks of Cap Blanc Nez and Cap Gris Nez. Everywhere, real life is played out against nature's most dramatic backdrops.

So much of the Dordogne and Périgord is hidden behind rich lush forests, but Rocamadour rises high and proud on a sheer limestone spur (above left). Clinging to the canyon this improbable village has flourished under the watchful eyes of eagles since the 12th century, when it was the site of countless pilgrimages to its black Madonna.

French for less than 200 years, the *nid d'aigle* (eagle's nest) village of Eze stands 1,410ft (43m) above sea level on a steep rocky crag overlooking the Côte d'Azur (above right). An outpost of the counts of Savoy, fortified in the 12th century, it passed on to the principality of Monaco, until its citizens voted to join France in the 19th century.

ROCK

The rippling vertical strata of the Rocher de la Baume (left), where the mountains of Provence meet those of Dauphiné, loom over the old red-roofed houses of Sisteron on the banks of the Durance river.

VILLAGES

Previous page: Four seasons in one. A sun-kissed meadow in the wild and beautiful Queyras Regional Park that sprawls across the Franco-Italian border is fringed by a forest decked out in the colors of fall, and dominated by the snow-capped peaks of the mountains.

As the high-speed trains run north to south so the changing shapes and forms of the villages mark out the miles. Wooden farmsteads and black slate in the north and west and sloping roofs with gables in the east.

The farther south, the flatter the roofs, and slate gives way to weather-burned terracotta. The red clay tops of the houses declare that you are traveling ever closer to the Midi, the land of the hot noonday sun.

From huge ports on the Channel, Atlantic, and Mediterranean mainland and simple little harbors on the islands that dot the coast, France hoists sail for the catch of the day.

Whether huge industrial factory ships that set out from Marseille and Boulogne, or those brightly painted blue and red wooden boats upturned on the beaches at St-Tropez and Wimereux where old men mend their nets, vessels go out to sea and land their prize at the harborside to be auctioned in time-honored fashion.

The open seas may yield their crops of seabass (known as *bar* in the north and *loup de mer* in the south), tuna and, more rarely with each season, cod. However, the bays and inlets of the coastal waters are natural farms for seafood and shellfish.

FISHING BOATS

Lobster pots are tended all around the country and, in Brittany and Aquitaine, Normandy, and Languedoc, oysters and mussels are harvested daily. Boatmen guide their flat-bottom *chaluts* around the tables of the oyster beds in the *étangs* (lakes) of the south, harvesting *huîtres de Bouzigues* from the crystal-clear waters of the Thau lagoon. Their Norman counterparts walk out at low tide to bring in the crop from St-Vaast-la-Hougue. Farmers in Brittany know that the bulk of their catch is reserved for the grandest tables of Paris, where masterchefs come up with ever more inventive ways of serving the cherished and sought-after *bélons* and *fines claires*.

France has a long seafaring tradition: *corsaires* once set sail from Dunkerque. These were privateers, semi-licensed pirates, out to plunder booty from other boats in the name of the king; men such as Jean Bart (1650–1702), long accorded folk-hero status, loved as the Robin Hoods of the seas.

COAST

The coasts have their modern heroes too. When the British solo round-the-world yachtswoman Ellen MacArthur arrived in port at Les Sables d'Olonne after 94 days at sea, thousands crowded the wharf. The coast is large enough to contain both hero-worshipers and the hedonists who flock to the casino-studded holiday resorts, and the health-seekers who enjoy seaweed wraps and power-spraying at thalassotherapy spas. Watersports have their place, but there are also many special settings for solitude and reflection: unspoiled beaches along countless inlets and coves blending improbably blue and violet waters with glimmering golden sunlight and lush green countryside as far as the eye can see.

PASTORAL

Straight, unending roads lined with tall trees making a gray-green tunnel of shade on the brightest summer's day; elderflowers, poppies, and brambles on the roadside against serried ranks of vines, rich threads of green against the dust of a dry afternoon; a patchwork of fields, civilization making its presence felt by the occasional church spire and glint of sunshine on a slow-moving tractor; the crack of a shotgun followed by the joyful barking of a dog, warning pheasants, rabbits, wild boar, and unwary visitors that the fall hunting season is underway; and, in the south, the transhumance, when shepherds nudge their sheep from winter to spring pastures. The countryside marks the slow progress of the seasons, just as the Suisse Normande (above) offers its infinite variety of greens in July and wraps them all in a blanket of snow come January.

HISTORIC PARIS

The old and the new: creating an improbable yet successful harmony, I. M. Pei's glass pyramid reflects the older buildings of the Louvre museum in Paris in a dazzling kaleidoscope of centuries and style.

Perfectly poised at the hub of the Etoile, the top of the avenue des Champs-Elysées looking down toward the royal heart of the city and up to the new business district of La Défense, Napoleon's imposing Arc de Triomphe hosts France's Tomb of the Unknown Soldier.

The meringue-shape domes of Sacré-Coeur, high above the city at the crest of Montmartre dominate the Parisian skyline even more than the Eiffel Tower. The basilica was completed in 1914 and consecrated after World War I.

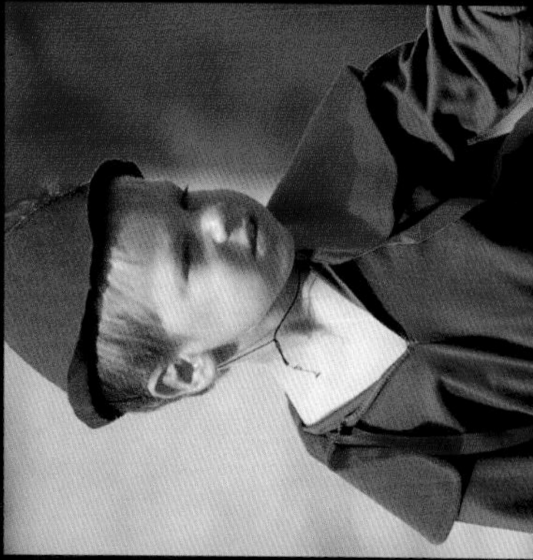

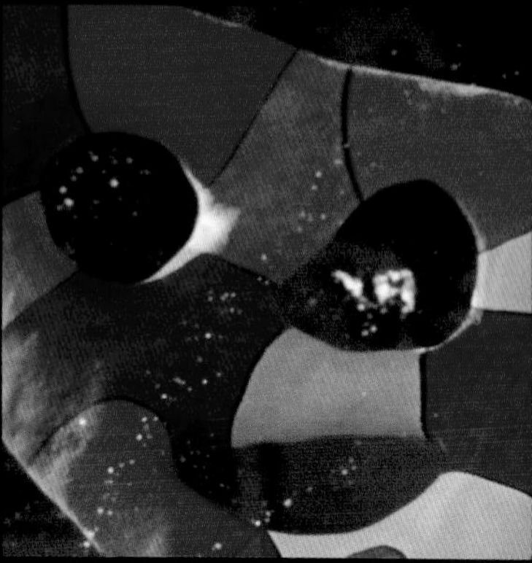

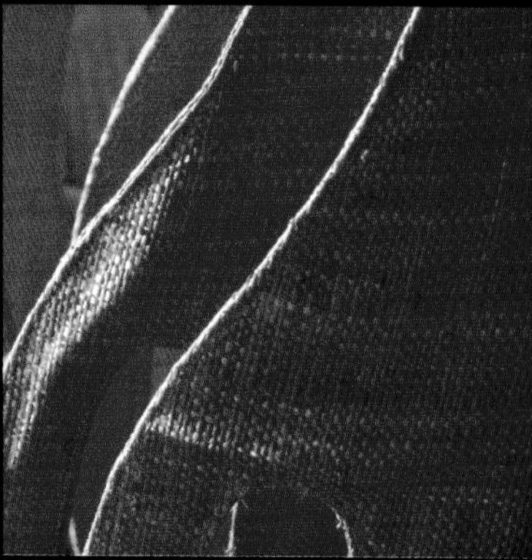

If cinema is *le 7ème art*, then surely *le 8ème* is shopping. The *grands magasins*, or department stores, each sprawling over several buildings and city blocks in the center of Paris, are laid out like art galleries with entire wings devoted to each theme. One floor for shoes, a specialist department for purses, and sometimes an entire shop devoted simply to beauty and pampering.

While the big prêt-à-porter fashion shows are sold out months in advance, the stores stage their own catwalk presentations for visitors several times a week, and the designer Pierre Cardin now has a purpose-built fashion theater in the capital's couture district.

Finding fashion under one roof is easy, especially with the services of in-store personal shoppers. However, the fun is in tracking down that special outfit or accessory for yourself. The couturiers

rue Royale - 75008 Paris - Tel.: 01 40 17 07 40
Bonaparte - 75006 Paris - Tel.: 01 56 24 15 60
www.swarovski.com

794 PDB 75

Flair and savoir-faire are the keynotes of French style. The same flourish is given to the click of an elegant heel on the sidewalk outside a chic boutique, as to the final signature of an artist on canvas, or the diva's acceptance of a bouquet at an opera-house curtain call.

If it is worth doing, do it with style, whether you are dressing up for a night on the town or building a cathedral. Do it with pride and do it with love.

have their salons and stylish shops, and designer boutiques flourish in Paris and towns around the country.
Every city has its smartest street where the established top labels and most sought-after store bags leave the shop doors. Yet university towns are

worth exploring further in order to discover the up and coming designers of the future in the less fashionable streets.
January and July see the annual *soldes* or sales when prices are gradually reduced through the four-to-six week season. The art is in judging

whether the initial 30–50 percent reduction is worth grabbing or to wait for the next drop in price and risk losing the cherished item.

The very streets of France are a canvas for the nation's artists. Against the improbable backdrop of bourgeois apartments, the 16th-century church of St-Merri, and Centre Georges Pompidou, the Stravinski Fountains in Beaubourg (above) are a burst of youthful enthusiasm.

A flamboyant figure on Nice's Promenade des Anglais (above right) evokes the city's famed February Mardi Gras carnival when papier-mâché creations, several stories high, are paraded through the streets before they are set alight at sea on the Baie des Anges.

Opposite: France's great sporting tradition celebrates its artistic side with Jean-Bernard Metais' sculptural evocation of the great Tour de France cycle race at Pau, scene of the event's tough Pyrenean stages.

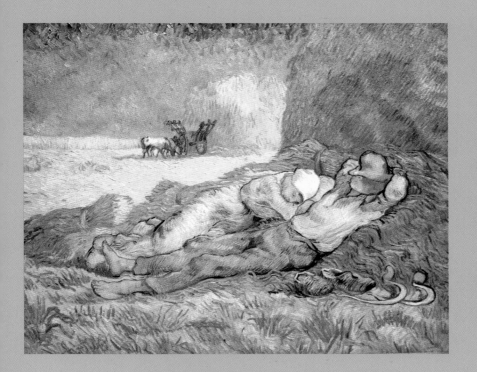

Opposite: Rodin's *The Thinker* in the gardens of the Musée-Rodin in Paris.

St-Rémy is where Vincent van Gogh spent a period of self-internment toward the end of his life and spent his hours in intensive painting. One such work *The Midday Siesta* (1889–1890) was copied from a drawing by Jean-François Millet. It is housed in the Musée d'Orsay.

Aix-en-Provence, like the life of its most famous resident Paul Cézanne, is dominated by the St-Victoire mountain, at different moments blue, gray, and even violet. The artist returned to the scene many times, most notably in this painting, dubbed simply *La Montagne Sainte-Victoire*.

Whenever and wherever France celebrates, one thing is certain: you are unlikely to go hungry or thirsty since the atmosphere is more family party than civic event, and, whatever the theme, glasses and plates are freely filled and refilled. Religion plays a strong part. In the east, St. Nicolas parades through town on December 6, the central European Santa offering children candy and gingerbread. Provence focuses on nativity scenes: craftsmen make clay figurines and shepherds lead their flocks to church on Christmas Eve. Easter sees Corsican processions of penitents.

Best known of the arts events, the Cannes Film Festival in May has the highest profile, but summer nights are filled with the sound of dying sopranos as countless Mimis and Violettas warble their last in open-air operas across the land. The biggest festival of all, Avignon, has a lively fringe

FESTIVALS

where the off and off-beat may be enjoyed on a basic budget.

Cultural serendipity is served best at such events as August's Périgord Noir season of unforgettable classical concerts in churches around the Dordogne. Art meets real life in St-Etienne's biennial contemporary design show: international innovation in couches, raincoats, lampshades, and tableware.

Traditional is sometimes a euphemism for off-beat and bizarre. In the south, towns have totemic animal emblems, huge chickens, bulls, and horses.

With origins lost in the mists of time, events such as the Soufflaculs parade in Nontron, Aquitaine, have to be witnessed to be disbelieved: villagers walk through town in their nightshirts, pumping bellows up each other's shirts in order to ward off evil spirits.

CHURCH ART

Works of art in themselves, from the great white spaces of Burgundy's Cistercian abbeys to the golden fiery splendor of Lourdes, the nation's churches house some spectacular artworks.

Through the centuries, artists and artisans have worked together to create vivid and powerful windows and altarpieces. Much statuary was destroyed or damaged in the wake of the Revolution, when religious icons were attacked by the mobs, but many powerful pieces remain.

In Salers, the polychrome stone entombment is in
the portal of the 15th-century St. Matthew's church
(top). The angel on the façade of Reims cathedral
is the city's symbol. The doors of Lille's Notre Dame
de la Treille feature a vine of human suffering
created by Holocaust survivor George Jeanclos.

pite the growth of out-of-town shopping malls

hypermarkets,

rish in the hear

ges boast a bo

tisserie (cake s

s a day.

OLORS OF F

In Brittany the traditional *crêperie* still thrives. The

butcher or cheese refiner, who prepares each

FLEURISTE

Crêperie

SIGNS

La Malouin

GOURMET

CRÊPERIE

They make knives in Bayonne (think of the word bayonet) and berets just a few miles from Lourdes. In Agde and Clermont l'Hérault, red and green pottery, with patterns of olives and crickets, is piled high in craft shops and on market stalls.

CRAFTS

Carpenters carve and chisel out wooden toys in Alsace for Strasbourg's renowned Christmas markets, and the best nativity creations of all are the *crèches* (cribs) with their hand-made *santons*, figurines of biblical and local characters created by the artists of Aubagne, outside Marseille.

December brings *foires aux santons* (Christmas exhibitions and sales) to towns and villages across the south, but summer sees midnight Marchés Nocturnes where craftspeople sell their wares under the stars.

LIGHT & REFLECT

COLORS OF FRANCE:

LIGHT & REFLECTIONS

ONS

6

RIVERS
& CANALS

Every new light, each sunset or strike of a match in the darkest night, brings a fresh perspective of a country that has a special private face it reveals to each visitor.

Find a glimpse of your own private France by the seashore at dawn, in the city at dusk, on a mid-afternoon trip down the river, fingers trailing in the water, or bathed in multicolored light in a centuries-old chapel.

Protected by the dappled shade of ancient trees whose gnarled and knotted roots shore up their banks, the canals and rivers are the silent arteries that link the mountains to the seas, the perfect setting for dreams.
One waterside visionary was Paul Riquet (1604–80), whose ambition of linking the Mediterranean to the Atlantic was made reality with his 17th-century Canal du Midi, now a UNESCO listed site. The simple, elegant waterway is in fact a triumph of engineering, with complex locks and aqueducts. These watery thoroughfares were worked hard.

Gabares, flat-bottom wooden boats, took cargoes of timber downstream to the coopers of Bordeaux, then the boats themselves would be chopped up as timber. Now these waterways are strictly for leisure; a couple pedal their way up the River Thouet by the gardens of Montreuil-Bellay (above).

WATER'S EDGE

France has its *rivières* and France has its *fleuves*. The former are rivers, modest or majestic in their own right, that meander through the countryside, fed by well-tempered tributaries from high gorges and gentle hills.

The latter, among them the Seine, the Somme, the Loire, and the Rhône, make their way undeterred to the seas, emerging in broad wide-mouthed estuaries such as Le Havre and Marseille. These engines of a nation are gateways between all that France has to offer and all the world has to share. The working ports, where fresh water meets the salty Mediterranean and Atlantic, give way to broad beaches stretching into infinite sunsets. Here people enjoy sand-yachting, fishing, walking for miles with the dog, or simply wandering alone, far from the workaday world, opening eyes and mind to the vistas of possibilities.

SAFE HARBOR

As the fishing boats put into port at Honfleur in Normandy (right), so Europe's only domestic flocks of flamingos settle on the saltwater lagoons of Languedoc-Roussillon (above), where their neighbors are egrets, herons, storks, and kingfishers.

The mystic and calming light of stained-glass windows dresses a church for prayer. Hues of blues, reds, and gold carpet the flagstone floors, their patterns passing imperceptibly with the invisible measured pace of the sun outside.

The bright splashes of light are nudged into seeming movement by the flickering light of a pyramid of votive candles, as flames dance in the breeze created with each opening of a side door. Each new rush of light refreshes for a second some corner, some feature of architectural gloom as a private revelation of beauty.

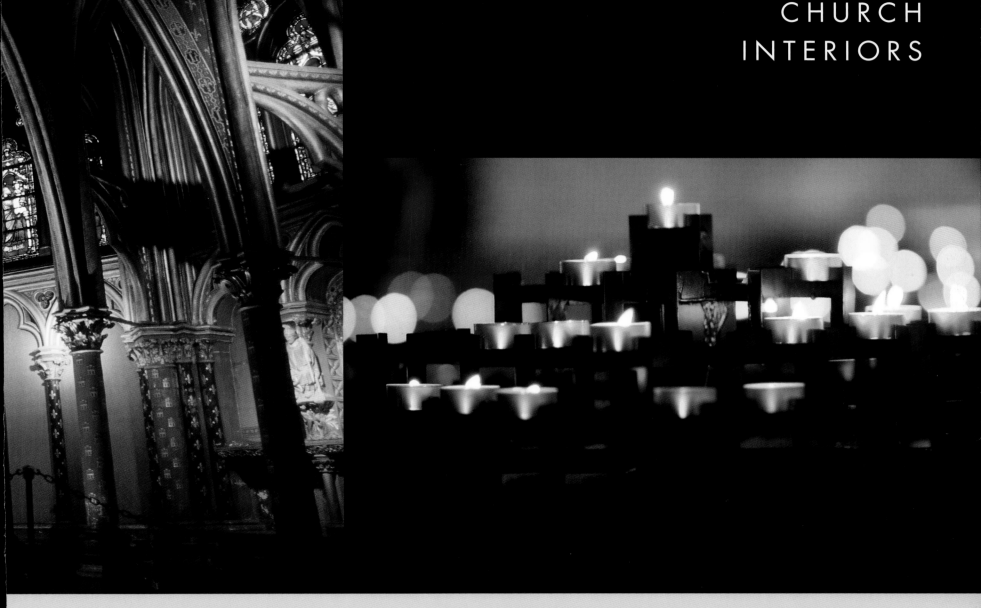

As eyes become accustomed to the gentle pastel-
anointed obscurity, so the original patchworks of
color begin to take shape and make sense.
Contemplation leads to recognition of a much-
loved Bible story, and the faces of the half-hidden
statuary regain familiarity in the calm half-light.

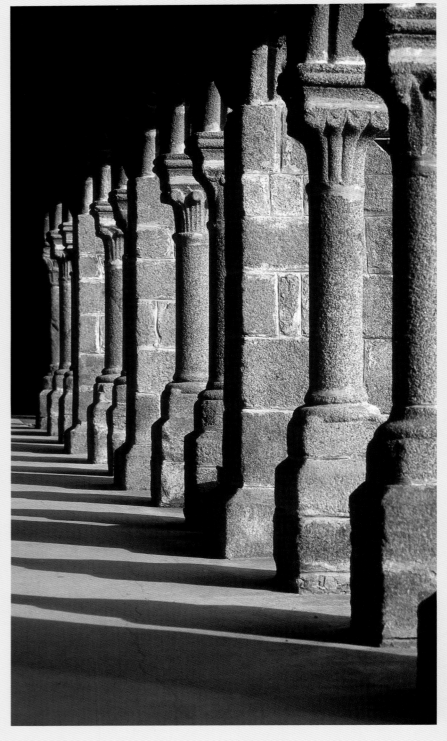

Normandy is the country of abbeys. Most famous of all, and as much a symbol of France as the Eiffel Tower, is the *merveille* that is Mont St-Michel, as permanent and everlasting as the granite rock on which it rises out of the bay. However, you could be forgiven for forgetting the Mont's monastic role when confronted with thousands of tourists in its narrow streets on a sunny day.

The region has plenty more sites for reflection. William the Conqueror (1027–87), Duke of Normandy and King of England (1066–87) built two abbeys by his castle in Caen to atone for an incestuous marriage. One monastery was for monks and one for nuns, the Abbaye aux Dames (far left).

Some abbeys were great hubs of learning. The wonderfully peaceful religious campus of Le Bec Hellouin regularly supplied England with Archbishops of Canterbury. Others were more modest places of contemplation, such as the romanesque Abbaye Blanche in Mortain (center).

The classic stillness of Rouen's cathedral (above), a frequent subject for the Impressionist artist Claude Monet (1840–1926), provides a Gothic contrast to the dramatic modern church of Joan of Arc, a few hundred yards across the city.

NIGHT LIGHT

Paris in the daytime is only resting. The City of Lights comes alive at night. Each of the great monuments is illuminated as a priceless jewel in a classic setting. Notre Dame reflected in the waters of the Seine (left); the Arc de Triomphe (center) a flaming torch that sets a string of light the length of the Champs-Elysées, complemented by the red and yellow headlamps and tail-lights of a thousand cars and the vivid colors spilling out onto the sidewalks from the stores and restaurants still bustling and busy round midnight; the Eiffel Tower (right), for generations content to loom as modest

dark-brown ironwork in the shadows, was dressed in thousands of light bulbs for the Paris millennium celebrations, and has brightened up the night sky ever since.

MIRRORS

France loves looking at itself, and it enjoys playing with its own reflection. So much of the new deliberately shines a light on its surroundings in tribute to what has gone before and nature's generous dowry.

A delicious political irony is the cluster of silvery balls in the courtyard of the Palais Royal that contort the smiles of visitors (above left). The irresistible image is that of the people's sport *boules* or *pétanque*, the leisure pursuit of the humble citizen in the gardens of a king.

Reflecting the skies and looking toward the future: the dazzling steel sphere of La Géode's IMAX cinema (above right) at the Parc de La Villette, the science and cultural center on the northern edge of Paris.

FOUNTAINS

Dancing jets of water splash the sunlight in extravagant fountains at place du Général de Gaulle in the spa town of Aix-en-Provence (above) and on the Esplanade des Quinconces in Bordeaux (right).

The wilful display of wasting water was long a symbol of a city's wealth. Not only could it afford to bring water to its people, so that they could drink and wash safely, it could afford to play with it as well.

Aix is known as the city of a hundred fountains. The city's Latin name was Aquae Sextiae, and since its founding, Aix has been synonymous with the refreshing sound of running water; four grand water-features stud the main thoroughfare, the Cours Mirabeau.

SEASONS **136**

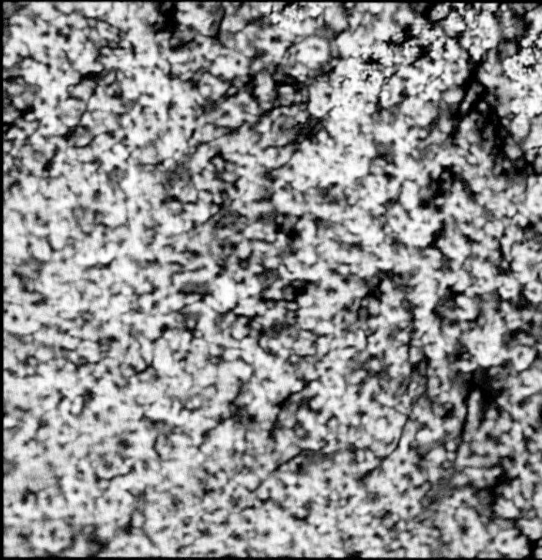

COLORS OF FRANCE: **TIME & MOTION**

SUMMER **140**

RURAL RETREAT **142**

France is a big country. Paris wears the same Chanel suits on the Faubourg St-Honoré as New York sports on Fifth Avenue and, her seasonal wardrobe is as wide as that of the United States. It may be a blustery March day in Paris, but there will be skiing in Chamonix and tanning in Cannes; sweater-sporting fishermen in Brittany are cousins to Irish Celts, just as Roussillon's Catalan musicians claim kinship with Pyrenean neighbors in Spain. Nobody should be surprised that, since the days of those black-and-white photographs, the frog has been kissed, the ugly truckling transformed into the celebrated high-speed T.G.V. (Train à Grande Vitesse). The map does not really prepare you for the culture shock as you zoom from region to region; now that journey times are so short, only climate changes remind you that a three-hour trip may have covered 725 miles (900km).

Once upon a time it was easy to recognize French railway carriages. They were serpentine, dark and dusty, bottle-green affairs, freezing in winter and stifling in the summer months. Four framed black-and-white photographs in each compartment gave the lie to your journey. If the picture showed a breathtaking alpine pass, you knew that the view through the window would feature the dusty *garrigue*. Should it offer Côte d'Azur beaches, the train would creak past inner-city graffiti.

Today, the dated photographs are gone, just as comfortable modern trains live up to their promises. You can hop on a train in the chill of the wintry north and step out onto a platform 800 miles (1,200km) south a few hours later to be mugged by the warmth of year-round sunshine.

The T.G.V. with air-conditioned expedience and efficiency pulls far-flung destinations within a commute of Paris, and even London. The superstars of the railway world, capable of traveling at 186mph (297kph), are flagships of a highly sophisticated rail network keeping the diverse strands of the nation on a central leash.

And as Europe opens up its network of no-frills budget airlines, and France itself unrolls ever more well-maintained *autoroutes* (freeways), mere remoteness is no longer a bar to exploration.

Grande vitesse is all very well, but some journeys need to be savored at a more leisurely pace: boat trips across to off-shore islands, for example, and longer ferry crossings to Corsica.

Two wheels have their place too: mountain bikes for exploring the countryside, scooters and Segway mobile platforms for getting around the city. Even the mailman negotiates the alleyways and back streets on a bicycle.

Out in the country, four legs outweigh even two wheels. Horseback riding is the best way to explore the byways of rural France. Where the terrain gets

tougher, the horse gives way to its more rugged cousin, the donkey.

Scottish writer Robert Louis Stevenson may be better known in the English-speaking world as the author of *Treasure Island* (1883), but in France he is universally loved for his *Travels With a Donkey in the Cevennes* (1879), an account of his trek through the stunning mountains, valleys, plateaus, and villages of the heartland.

Each year, hundreds of people follow his journey, paperback in backpack or downloaded e-book in palmtop, hiring donkeys to be stabled overnight at the inns, *gîtes* (self-catering), and *chambres d'hôte* (bed-and-breakfast) accommodations on the route through Lozère and beyond.

24 HOURS

From dawn to shimmering dawn, each moment is there to be appreciated. Daybreak over Sacré Coeur in Paris, Mont St-Michel in Normandy (left), or Notre Dame de la Garde in Marseille, the sunrise silhouette is but the first possibility of the day or the final curtain-call of an unforgettable night.

In Paris the night sky is hidden by the neon of Pigalle's dance halls and cabarets. The city is best seen during the weekly roller marathon, when thousands of bladers and skaters gather round midnight for a mass ride, a free-wheeling cheer of humanity whizzing down the Champs-Elysées.

Others take their Paris by night alone or à *deux*. Watching the sleepy river from the tip of the Île St-Louis, warming themselves with the first fresh-baked croissant from a Left Bank bakery, or toasting the night that's passed with onion soup at dawn in a market café in Les Halles.

France awakens from winter with the watery eyed realization of spring. Low-lying cloud floats over the town of Chamonix, nestling in the Arve Valley (above); the peaks and glaciers of the Mont-Blanc massif towering in the background.

The only sign of life, as the last winter sun begins to tease the snow from the tips of the trees lining a narrow single-track road along a forest trail are the tire tracks that prove somebody's day has already begun.

SEASONS

In the far south, a sprinkling of white is a sign of
spring and not winter, when blossom appears as if
by magic on the boughs of the almond and fruit
trees that punctuate the vast spreading vineyards
of Languedoc and Provence.

SUMMER

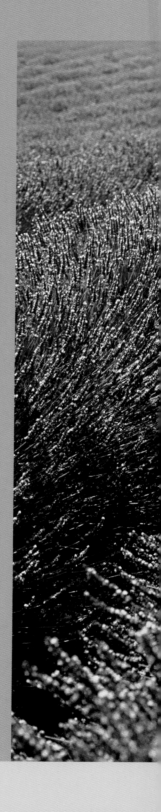

The south may dress in the gray and rust colors of the garrigue scrubland for so much of the year—browns, golds, and beiges, lightened by the muted shades of sage, thyme, and rosemary. But with the summer come the brightest colors: cornflowers, poppies, and dandelions dance in the hedgerows.

Best of all, in the Luberon and across Provence, endless fields of lavender stretch as far as the eye can see, row after row of violet light misting in the sun and creating a purple-toned horizon.

Orchids and butterflies, wild deer and songbirds await those who head away from the city at the end of a week of bustle and commitment. By the lake or in the mountains, on the coast or in the woods, contentment is but a short drive out of town.

Some come for the comforts of manicured lawns and tended window boxes at a weekender chalet with overhanging eaves and wooden balconies— a hub of activity during the ski season but a haven of peace at other times, such as this retreat in Sixt Fer-à-Cheval in Haute-Savoie (above).

RURAL RETREAT

Others plan to lose themselves in the pattern of
fall colors that evolves as green turns to gold,
brown, and yellow in the national and regional
parks and forests of Queyras and Périgord,
Normandie-Maine and Grands Causses, Anjou
and Haute-Corbières.

CREDITS

The photographs used inside this book are held in the Automobile Association's own photo library **(AA World Travel Library)** and were taken by the following photographers:

Adrian Baker 27b, 31tr, 72bl, 74r, 75; **Pete Bennett** 12/3, 42t, 48/9, 51c, 52l, 62l, 62b, 63, 102b; **Ian Dawson** 31br, 44/5, 87, 108bc, 108br, 112, 113t, 114/5, 118l, 119; **Roger Day** 56r, 65t; **Steve Day** 80tl, 81bl, 105b; **Jerry Edmanson** 3cr, 35l, 72br, 81tl, 91br, 107l, 107r; **Philip Enticknap** 54bl, 58/9, 135t; **Debbie Ireland** 96r; **Paul Kenward** 5bcr, 10cr, 16r, 17, 20t, 28t, 29r, 51l, 54br, 62t, 78t, 85cl, 90br, 100tl, 100bl, 100br, 101tl, 101tr, 101bl, 101br, 104tr, 104b, 105tl, 105tr, 108bl, 110t, 111, 138/9; **Alex Kouprianoff** 4bc, 4br, 5bl, 24, 30tr, 37br, 47r, 53, 54bc, 55bc, 60l, 60r, 61, 66c, 68t, 73bl, 80bl, 81r, 83, 91bl, 103, 113b, 133l, 133r; **Max Jourdan** 30cb, 35r, 36bc, 38l, 39l, 39t, 39b, 40l, 40r, 55bl, 73bc, 86l, 92l, 93l, 93r, 125l, 128bl, 130cr, 130b, 131t; **Eric Meacher** 3tl, **Rob Moore** 8/9, 29br, 30br, 41r, 50c, 52b, 55br, 64b, 65cr, 66l, 70/1, 72bc, 78bl, 79, 84tl, 84tr, 84br, 85c, 102t, 110b, 118r, 142r;

Roger Moss 28b, 78r; **Tony Oliver** 20cr, 84c, 142l; **Ken Paterson** 99r, 116/7; **Neil Ray** 16l; **Bertrand Rieger** 123; **Clive Sawyer** 5bcl, 5br, 6, 10bl, 11l, 11r, 18bl, 18bc, 20cl, 21t, 21b, 22/3, 25t, 30tl, 31tl, 31c, 36bl, 37bc, 38b, 50r, 64c, 65b, 67c, 69, 82r, 90bl, 90bc, 92r, 94tl, 94tr, 94c, 94bl, 94bc, 94br, 95tl, 95tr, 95c, 95bc, 95br, 96l, 114, 117, 128bc, 129bl, 130t, 132tr, 134, 140/1, 144; **Neil Setchfield** 4bl, 18br, 19br, 26tl, 26b, 26r, 27tr, 30bl, 34l, 36br, 41l, 41c, 42l, 57r, 65c, 66bl, 68r, 74l, 85cr, 97, 124, 127, 131b, 132tl; **Michael Short** 3tr, 19bc, 27tl, 33t, 33b, 109bl, 116; **Barrie Smith** 14/5, 25b, 34r, 47l, 51r, 85t, 128br, 135b, 137; **Tony Souter** 3tcl, 32, 38t, 57l, 67l, 99l, 122, 122/3, **Rick Strange** 37bl, 40c, 42b, 43l, 43r, 46t, 46b, 50l, 52r, 64l, 76/7, 80r, 82l, 86r, 100tr, 106, 109br, 126, 129bc, 143; **James Tims** 73br, 88, 88/9, 89, 109bc, 112/3, 125r; **Roy Victor** 60/1; **John White** 136l, 136r; **Jon Wyand** 19bl, 29l, 64tr.